The World of Artificial intelligence

Exploring the Future of Technology and Innovation

Robert M. Starnes

TABLE OF CONTENTS

---

[1]

INTRODUCTION

In the annals of human civilization, a phenomenon has developed that has the capacity to transform the world as we know it—Artificial Intelligence, or AI. As the digital age drives us into unexplored realms of technological innovation, AI is at the vanguard, promising to alter the way we live, work, and interact. It is a domain where robots replicate human cognitive processes, unraveling intricacies and uncovering possibilities that long lived entirely inside the realm of science fiction.

AI symbolizes the aim of building intelligent agents, systems that can observe, reason, learn, and act, frequently exceeding human capabilities. From analyzing detailed patterns within enormous datasets to making judgments based on probabilistic reasoning, AI exceeds the boundaries of conventional programming and delves into the world of autonomous learning. It's the force driving self-driving vehicles, allowing virtual assistants to grasp our orders, and powering recommendation algorithms that define our online experiences.

But AI is not only a technical wonder; it's a driver for innovation across disciplines. It spans the divide between what was formerly believed unbelievable and what is now on the edge of reality. It has spurred arguments about ethics, privacy, and the future of labor. It has joined computer scientists, mathematicians, ethicists, and artists in a common path toward unlocking the full potential of intelligent machines.

This investigation into the domain of AI is a trip into the unknown, where we unearth the inner workings of algorithms that govern our digital world, navigate the ethical challenges that accompany this power, and picture a future where AI and humans live together. It's a voyage where the borders between the conceivable and the impossible blur, where the combination of human brilliance and technology power drives us into the unexplored frontiers of development.

As we begin on our voyage across the terrain of AI, let us peep into the algorithms that interpret languages, grasp the complexity of neural networks that imitate the human brain, and dig into the ethical issues that set the bounds of AI's potential. Let us celebrate the advances that have led us here and consider the future that AI promises to produce. The age of AI is coming, and with it, we find ourselves on the threshold of a new era—a future where the unlikely becomes reality, and the unfathomable becomes normal.

CHAPTER 1

What is Artificial Intelligence?

1.1 Defining Artificial Intelligence (AI)

Artificial Intelligence(AI), is an edge field in computer science that aims to create intelligent machines that are capable of performing tasks or work that are typically based on human intelligence. In essence, AI seeks to replicate human cognitive functions, allowing computers and machines to learn, reason, solve problems, and make decisions in ways that mimic human thought processes.

Replicating Human Intelligence

At its core, AI seeks to imbue machines with the ability to think and act intelligently, enabling them to analyze complex situations, adapt to changing circumstances, and generate appropriate responses. This is achieved through the creation of algorithms and systems that simulate various aspects of human cognition, enabling machines to perform tasks that were previously considered exclusive to human beings.

Cognitive Capacities and AI Applications

The scope of AI encompasses a wide range of cognitive capacities that define human intelligence. These include:

Learning: AI systems are designed to learn from experience and data. They can identify patterns, extract insights, and adapt their behavior based on the information they acquire. Machine learning, a subset of AI, focuses on developing algorithms that enable computers to improve their performance over time by learning from data.

Reasoning: AI systems can perform logical reasoning, deducing conclusions from available information. This capability allows machines to process complex information and make informed decisions based on logical principles.

Problem-Solving: AI algorithms excel at solving intricate problems, often through a process of trial and error. They can navigate through various solutions and select the most suitable one based on predefined criteria.

Decision-Making: AI systems are capable of making decisions based on data analysis and predefined rules. These decisions can range from simple choices to complex strategic moves.

Data Processing and Pattern Recognition

A significant aspect of AI is its ability to process vast amounts of data. AI systems can analyze large datasets at unprecedented speeds, detecting patterns and relationships that may not be apparent to human observers. This capability is particularly valuable in fields such as finance, healthcare, and marketing, where insights gleaned from data analysis can drive informed decisions and strategies.

Predictions and Recommendations

AI's data-driven approach allows it to make predictions and recommendations based on the patterns it identifies. For example, AI algorithms can predict stock market trends, suggest personalized content on streaming platforms, or recommend products to online shoppers based on their preferences and browsing history.

In essence, AI represents the frontier of computer science, where machines are becoming progressively more adept at performing tasks that were once the exclusive domain of human intelligence. As AI continues to advance, it holds the potential to revolutionize industries, enhance human productivity, and reshape the way we interact with technology in our daily lives.

1.2   Historical   Overview   of   Artificial Intelligence

Ancient Roots of AI: Legends and Philosophical Debates

The journey of Artificial Intelligence (AI) traces back to ancient legends and philosophical discussions about creating intelligent beings. In mythology, tales of automata and golems were early expressions of humanity's fascination with the idea of bringing non-human entities to life. Philosophers like Aristotle contemplated the nature of thought and reasoning, laying the groundwork for discussions about what it means for a machine to possess intelligence.

The Dawn of Modern AI: Early Concepts and Turing's Influence

The emergence of modern AI can be attributed to the development of digital computers and the theoretical contributions of mathematicians and scientists. In the mid-20th century, Alan Turing's pioneering work on computability and the concept of a "universal machine" laid the foundation for the idea that a machine could replicate human cognitive processes.

The Dartmouth Workshop (1956) and Birth of AI

A pivotal moment in the history of AI occurred in the summer of 1956 with the Dartmouth Workshop, led by John McCarthy, Marvin Minsky, Nathaniel Rochester, and Claude Shannon. This event marked the formal establishment of AI as a field of study. Attendees believed that computers had the potential to simulate human intelligence and tackle complex problems. This era was characterized by optimism and the expectation that AI systems would soon exhibit human-like abilities.

The Rise and Fall: Multiple Waves of AI Evolution

1. The Age of Symbolic AI (1956-1974): In the early years, AI research focused on symbolic reasoning, using formal logic to represent knowledge and solve problems.

This approach achieved notable successes, including the creation of expert systems that could mimic human expertise in specific domains.

2. The Birth of Machine Learning (1980s-1990s): The emergence of machine learning algorithms marked a shift in AI research. Researchers began developing systems that could learn from data, adapting their behavior based on experience. Neural networks, genetic algorithms, and other techniques paved the way for AI systems to improve over time.

3. The Era of "AI Winters" (1970s-1980s and 1990s-2000s): Despite early enthusiasm, AI faced periods of skepticism and reduced funding known as "AI winters." These periods were marked by overhyped expectations that didn't align with technological capabilities at the time. However, each "winter" eventually gave way to renewed interest and breakthroughs.

Contemporary AI: Resurgence and Advancements

The 21st century has witnessed a remarkable resurgence in AI research and application. Breakthroughs in machine learning, particularly deep learning, have enabled AI systems to achieve remarkable feats, from image recognition to natural language processing. This has led to the proliferation of AI-powered technologies in various industries, including healthcare, finance, transportation, and entertainment.

Conclusion

The history of AI is a story of visionaries who dared to imagine machines that could think, reason, and learn. From ancient myths to modern technologies, the journey has been marked by moments of hope, challenges, and persistent innovation. As AI continues to evolve, its impact on society and the way we interact with technology is destined to shape the future in ways that once seemed unimaginable.

1.3 Importance and Impact of Artificial Intelligence

AI: A Transformative Force in Modern Society

The significance of Artificial Intelligence (AI) in today's society cannot be overstated. AI has emerged as a transformative force that has the potential to reshape various facets of human life, from industries and economies to the way we interact with technology and make decisions. This chapter delves into the profound impact of AI across diverse sectors, highlighting both its promise and the ethical considerations it brings to the forefront.

Revolutionizing Industries

AI's influence spans across industries, and its applications have the power to revolutionize how businesses operate. In healthcare, AI-driven diagnostics and predictive analytics are improving patient outcomes, while AI-powered robots enhance efficiency in manufacturing processes. In finance, algorithms analyze vast amounts of data to make informed investment decisions, and in entertainment, recommendation systems personalize content consumption for users.

Healthcare Advancements

One of the most compelling examples of AI's impact is within the field of healthcare. AI-powered diagnostic tools are able to analyze medical images and detect abnormalities with high accuracy. For instance, AI algorithms have been developed to identify signs of diseases like cancer from X-rays and MRIs, leading to earlier detection and treatment. This technology has the potential to save lives by catching diseases at their earliest stages when they are most treatable.

Autonomous Vehicles and Transportation

AI's potential to transform the transportation sector is evident through the development of autonomous vehicles. These vehicles utilize advanced sensors, machine learning algorithms, and real-time data processing to navigate roads, making driving safer and more efficient. The integration of AI in transportation extends to traffic management, reducing congestion and enhancing urban mobility.

Ethical and Societal Considerations

As AI's reach expands, it brings with it a set of ethical and societal considerations. The displacement of jobs due to automation is a concern, necessitating the need for workforce reskilling and upskilling. Bias and discrimination in AI systems are also points of contention, as algorithms trained on biased data can perpetuate inequalities. The importance of responsible AI research and the need for transparency in algorithms and decision-making processes are crucial to addressing these concerns.

Real-World Examples

Throughout this chapter, real-world examples illustrate the practical impact of AI. AI-driven virtual assistants like Siri and Alexa have become integral parts of many households, demonstrating the convenience and capabilities that AI offers. On a grander scale, AI-enabled systems in autonomous vehicles showcase how advanced technologies are reshaping the future of transportation.

Conclusion

In conclusion, the importance and impact of AI are undeniable. From transforming industries to revolutionizing healthcare and transportation, AI is a force that is shaping the present and future of human society. Understanding the potential of AI and the ethical considerations it raises is crucial as we navigate a world increasingly intertwined with intelligent machines. This chapter provides a comprehensive exploration of AI's impact, leaving readers with a clear understanding of its significance and its potential to reshape our modern environment.

CHAPTER 2

Foundations of AI

2.1 Machine Learning Techniques

Introduction to Machine Learning

Machine Learning (ML) is a crucial subset of Artificial Intelligence that allows computers to better their performance on certain tasks by learning from data. It significantly modifies how computers interpret information by allowing them to automatically recognize patterns, derive insights, and generate predictions based on the data they have been exposed to. This section goes into the depths of machine learning, covering its methodology, principles, and famous algorithms.

Supervised Learning: Learning from Labeled Data

Supervised learning is a core notion in machine learning, where algorithms are trained on a labeled dataset. This dataset consists of input data coupled with matching labels or results. The aim is for the algorithm to understand the mapping between inputs and outputs, allowing it to make accurate predictions on fresh, unknown data. Algorithms prominent in supervised learning include vector support machines, trees of decision and neural networks.

Unsupervised Learning: Discovering Hidden Patterns

Unsupervised learning includes collecting patterns and insights from data without any labeled outcomes. In this strategy, the algorithm detects intrinsic patterns within the data, such as grouping similar data points together. Clustering methods like k-means and hierarchical clustering come under this category. Dimensionality reduction approaches, such principal component analysis (PCA), aid in reducing large datasets while keeping their key properties.

Reinforcement Learning: Learning Through Interaction

Reinforcement learning is a dynamic strategy where an agent learns to execute behaviors within an environment to maximize a cumulative reward. The agent gets feedback based on its behaviors, enabling it to develop optimum methods over time. This approach is widespread in training autonomous systems, such as self-driving vehicles and game-playing AI. Reinforcement learning incorporates concepts like states, actions, rewards, and policies to direct learning.

Key Concepts in Machine Learning

Training Data: The dataset used to train a machine learning model, containing input characteristics and matching labels or outputs.

Features: These are the features or properties of the input data that the model utilizes to create predictions. The choice of features considerably effects the model's performance.

Labels: In supervised learning, labels are the expected results associated with input data. They are used to train the algorithm how to produce correct predictions.

Model Evaluation: Assessing the performance of a machine learning model using measures such as accuracy, precision, recall, and F1-score. Cross-validation is a method used to validate the model's generalizability.

Prominent Algorithms

Decision Trees: A tree-like structure that makes judgments based on feature values, branching along multiple pathways to obtain results.

Support Vector Machines (SVM): A classification method that identifies the best hyperplane to distinguish various classes with the largest margin.

K-Nearest Neighbors (KNN): An algorithm that classifies data points based on the majority class of their k-nearest neighbors in the feature space.

In essence, machine learning revolutionizes how computers learn and adapt by automating the process of information extraction from data. From supervised learning for precise predictions to unsupervised learning for finding hidden structures, and reinforcement learning for training dynamic systems, machine learning methods are influencing industries and driving innovation across numerous areas.

2.2 Neural Networks and Deep Learning

Introduction to Neural Networks

Neural networks are at the core of recent developments in Artificial Intelligence, notably in the area of deep learning. These networks are inspired by the structure and operation of the human brain, with linked nodes (neurons) that process and send information. The chapter discusses the principles of neural networks, their components, and the tremendous influence they have on diverse AI applications.

Neural Network Structure and Operation

Neural networks consist of layers of linked nodes, each carrying learnable weights and biases. These nodes imitate the activity of neurons, accepting input, processing it, and creating output. Activation functions within nodes introduce non-linearity, allowing the network to understand complicated correlations within data. The connections between nodes, or synapses, are allocated weights that alter during training to maximize the network's performance.

Convolutional Neural Networks (CNNs) for Image Processing

Convolutional Neural Networks (CNNs) are a specific sort of neural network optimized for image processing applications. They employ convolutional layers to automatically recognize elements like edges, textures, and patterns inside pictures. By learning hierarchical representations of information, CNNs can perform tasks like picture categorization, object identification, and face recognition with outstanding accuracy.

Recurrent Neural Networks (RNNs) for Sequence Data

Recurrent Neural Networks (RNNs) are intended to handle sequential data, making them useful for applications requiring sequences, such as natural language processing and time series analysis. The feature loops that enable information to be transmitted from one stage of the network to the next is RNNs Long Short-Term Memory (LSTM) and Gated Recurrent Unit (GRU) are variations of RNNs that handle the difficulty of disappearing gradients, allowing the network to preserve long-range relationships.

Deep Learning and Applications

Deep Learning is a subset of machine learning that utilizes deep neural networks with several layers. These layers enable the network to learn detailed patterns and representations in data, making them well-suited for difficult tasks. Deep learning's applications stretch across disciplines including computer vision, natural language processing, voice recognition, and autonomous systems. For instance, deep learning has changed picture production, language translation, and even allowed advancements in self-driving automobiles.

2.3 Natural Language Processing (NLP)

Introduction to Natural Language Processing

Natural Language Processing (NLP) is a discipline of AI devoted to bridging the gap between human language and machine comprehension. It comprises tools and approaches that allow computers to interpret, analyze, and produce human language. NLP has the key to transforming communication between people and robots.

Challenges of Language Processing

Language is intrinsically complicated, having complexities in syntax, semantics, and context. NLP addresses issues including sentiment analysis, where computers detect the emotional tone of text, and named entity identification, which recognizes items like names, dates, and places inside text. Understanding language entails disambiguating meanings and accounting for context.

NLP Methodologies and Applications

NLP approaches include sentiment analysis, which assesses emotions in text, and machine translation, which transforms text from one language to another. Chatbots, fueled by NLP, replicate human speech and find applications in customer service and virtual assistants. Language models like BERT and GPT-3 have pushed NLP to new heights, allowing more natural and context-aware interactions.

Transformation of Human-Computer Interaction

NLP's significance extends to human-computer interaction, where voice assistants like Siri and Alexa have become fundamental aspects of everyday life. Chatbots offer rapid answers and suggestions, boosting user experiences. As NLP algorithms progress, they bridge the gap between human expression and computer comprehension, transforming how humans engage with technology.

In conclusion, neural networks, deep learning, and natural language processing are crucial in constructing the present AI environment. Neural networks allow the reproduction of complicated cognitive activities, while deep learning's hierarchical representations open the possibility for tackling sophisticated problems. Natural language processing promotes communication and interaction between people and machines, revolutionizing industries and defining the future of technology.

By the conclusion of this chapter, readers should have a basic knowledge of the key ideas that underlie AI, including machine learning methods, neural networks, and natural language processing. The chapter presents readers with the key knowledge required to study deeper into the diverse uses and implications of AI in subsequent chapters.

CHAPTER 3

AI in Everyday Life

3.1 AI in Virtual Assistants

Introduction to AI-Powered Virtual Assistants

AI has made tremendous advancements in producing virtual assistants that replicate human-like interactions and adapt to users' demands. This section discusses how AI technologies fuel virtual assistants like Siri, Alexa, and Google Assistant, altering the way we interact with our gadgets.

Voice Recognition and Natural Language Understanding

The core of virtual assistants resides in their capacity to recognize and interpret human speech. Voice recognition technology translates spoken words into text, while natural language understanding algorithms extract meaning and purpose from that text. These technologies allow users to speak with virtual assistants using natural language, making interactions more intuitive and user-friendly.

Context-Awareness and Personalization

AI-driven virtual assistants excel in context-awareness, recognizing not just the spoken words but also the context in which they are expressed. This helps them to give relevant and customised replies. For example, a virtual assistant may detect a user's location, preferences, and past interactions to make suggestions suited to their requirements.

Integration into Daily Routines

Virtual assistants have easily incorporated into our everyday lives, providing great support for many jobs. They help create reminders, answer enquiries, manage calendars, and even operate smart home gadgets. Their adaptability makes them a crucial tool for productivity, information retrieval, and hands-free multitasking.

3.2 AI in Social Media and Recommendations

AI in Social Media Platforms

The incorporation of AI in social media platforms has transformed how we engage with material and connect with people. AI systems monitor user behavior, interests, and interactions to create tailored content streams. This technology allows platforms to show users with material that matches with their tastes, keeping them interested and driving deeper connections.

Recommendation Engines: Personalizing User Experience

Recommendation engines, enabled by AI, are the backbone of content distribution on platforms like streaming services and e-commerce websites. These engines examine users' prior data and activity to forecast their preferences, proposing movies, goods, or material that corresponds with their inclinations. The outcome is a more engaging and user-centric experience.

Ethical Considerations and Challenges

The emergence of AI-powered recommendations presents ethical problems, such as the establishment of "filter bubbles," where users are exposed solely to material that validates their current ideas. There's also the question of data privacy and the possibility for algorithms to alter user behavior and attitudes. Striking a balance between personalisation and the variety of information becomes crucial to prevent any harmful repercussions.

AI's inclusion into virtual assistants and social media platforms has revolutionized how we interact with technology and engage with information. From natural voice interactions to tailored content suggestions, AI boosts convenience and tailors experiences to individual tastes. However, as AI continues to alter our digital experiences, careful consideration of ethical implications is important to ensure that these technologies serve the greater good without unwittingly perpetuating prejudices or restricting exposure to various viewpoints.

3.3 AI in Healthcare and Medicine

Introduction to AI in Healthcare

Artificial Intelligence (AI) has emerged as a game-changer in the healthcare business, transforming how medical practitioners diagnose, treat, and manage different ailments. This section addresses the far-reaching influence of AI in healthcare, from medical image analysis to patient care and pharmaceutical research.

Medical Image Processing and Diagnosis

AI-powered algorithms excel at processing medical pictures, such as X-rays, MRIs, and CT scans. These algorithms can swiftly identify abnormalities, detect early indicators of illnesses, and aid radiologists in making correct diagnosis. For instance, AI may recognize small changes in medical imaging that could go unnoticed by the human eye, leading to early treatments and better patient outcomes.

Pharmaceutical Research and Drug Discovery

AI is changing pharmaceutical research by expediting drug discovery methods. Machine learning algorithms examine huge datasets to find possible medication candidates, forecast their efficacy, and simulate their interactions with biological systems. This method expedites the drug development pipeline, cutting costs and boosting the possibilities of identifying novel medicines.

Personalized Medicine and Treatment Plans

AI allows the practice of customized medicine by evaluating patients' genetic, medical, and lifestyle data to adapt treatment strategies. This technique optimizes medicines for specific individuals, reducing adverse effects and boosting therapeutic success. AI-driven prediction models can estimate illness development, supporting physicians in making educated choices regarding patient treatment.

Obstacles and Potential in AI-Driven Healthcare

Regulatory Concerns and Data Privacy

The integration of AI in healthcare creates regulatory obstacles, since medical equipment and algorithms must comply to strict safety and efficacy criteria. Ensuring patient data privacy and ensuring the security of sensitive medical information are essential challenges in deploying AI-driven solutions.

Human-AI Collaboration and Specialist Interaction

AI systems in healthcare are meant to aid medical personnel rather than replace them. Ensuring efficient communication between AI systems and human professionals is vital. The problem comes in building AI systems that deliver actionable insights while being transparent and interpretable, allowing medical experts to make well-informed judgments.

Real-World Examples and Case Studies

AI's influence on healthcare is shown via real-world applications. IBM's Watson for Oncology examines medical literature and clinical trial data to offer tailored cancer therapy options. Google's DeepMind has created algorithms that can detect eye disorders from retinal scans, facilitating early diagnosis and management.

Conclusion

AI's transformational influence on healthcare and medicine is enormous. From identifying illnesses to expediting drug development and tailoring treatment strategies, AI is increasing patient care and transforming medical procedures. While issues connected to legislation and data protection exist, the potential advantages of AI-driven healthcare solutions are evident. This chapter presents readers with an in-depth overview of how AI is transforming the healthcare sector, eventually leading to greater patient outcomes and more efficient medical procedures.

CHAPTER 4

Ethical Considerations in AI

4.1 Bias and Fairness in AI

Introduction to Bias in AI Systems

As Artificial Intelligence (AI) becomes increasingly integrated into our daily lives, concerns about bias and fairness have come to the forefront. This section delves into the critical issue of bias in AI systems, exploring how biases can inadvertently creep into AI algorithms through biased training data and flawed design practices.

Biased Training Data and Inadequate Design

AI systems learn from data, and if that data is biased, the resulting algorithms can perpetuate and amplify those biases. Biased training data can result from historical inequalities or human prejudices, leading to skewed representations of various groups. Inadequate design, where the potential for bias is not considered during algorithm development, can exacerbate this problem.

Real-World Examples of Bias in AI

Several high-profile instances have highlighted the presence of bias in AI systems. Facial recognition technologies have exhibited racial bias, misidentifying individuals with darker skin tones more frequently. Sentencing algorithms used in criminal justice systems have demonstrated bias against minority defendants. These examples underscore the real-world consequences of biased AI systems, reinforcing existing societal inequalities.

Unfair Outcomes and Maintaining Inequities

When AI systems produce biased outputs, they can perpetuate discriminatory practices and widen societal inequities. Biased algorithms can reinforce stereotypes, exclude marginalized groups, and exacerbate disparities in areas such as hiring, lending, and access to services.

This threatens the principle of equal treatment and undermines the potential benefits of AI.

Strategies for Bias Discovery and Mitigation

To address bias in AI systems, strategies must be employed at various stages:

Data Auditing: Regularly reviewing training data for biases and taking corrective actions, such as re-sampling or introducing diversity.

Algorithm Auditing: Evaluating the outcomes of AI algorithms on different demographic groups to identify disparate impacts.

De-biasing Techniques: Implementing methods that reduce bias during algorithm training, ensuring equitable treatment for all groups.

Significance of Fairness and Diversity

Ensuring fairness and diversity in AI research and development is crucial. Diversity in the teams building AI systems can help mitigate bias, as diverse perspectives are more likely to recognize and address biases. Fairness in AI algorithms is essential to prevent discriminatory outcomes, promote ethical AI, and ensure that technology benefits everyone.

Conclusion

Addressing bias and promoting fairness in AI is a pressing concern for society. As AI technologies continue to evolve, ensuring that algorithms are equitable and unbiased is paramount. By acknowledging the potential for bias, actively working to uncover and mitigate it, and fostering diverse and inclusive AI research practices, we can strive to create AI systems that contribute positively to society without perpetuating harmful biases and inequities.

4.2 Privacy and Data Security in the Age of AI

Introduction to Privacy and Data Security

As Artificial Intelligence (AI) continues to permeate various aspects of our lives, the ethical implications surrounding data privacy and security become increasingly significant. This section explores the intricate interplay between AI systems and the vast amounts of data they rely upon, delving into issues related to data harvesting, storage, potential exploitation, and the ethical dilemmas that arise.

Data-Centric Nature of AI

AI systems thrive on data, particularly vast and diverse datasets. Whether it's training algorithms, improving performance, or making predictions, data is the fuel that powers AI's capabilities. However, this reliance on data also raises concerns about how this data is collected, stored, and potentially used to infer sensitive information about individuals.

Data Harvesting and Privacy Concerns

The collection of data often occurs seamlessly as individuals engage with technology, be it through social media, online shopping, or IoT devices. This data, though seemingly innocuous, can be combined to paint a detailed picture of an individual's preferences, behaviors, and even personal life. Privacy concerns arise as this data can be used to make inferences, expose vulnerabilities, and potentially compromise individual autonomy.

Balancing Data-Driven Insights and Privacy Rights

The tension between leveraging data for valuable insights and respecting individuals' privacy rights is at the heart of the AI and data security discourse. Striking the right balance is essential to ensure that technology advancements do not come at the cost of personal privacy. This requires transparent data collection practices, informed consent, and robust safeguards against unauthorized access.

Legislation and Regulation

In response to the challenges posed by data privacy, legislation such as the General Data Protection Regulation (GDPR) in Europe and the California Consumer Privacy Act (CCPA) in the United States has been enacted. These regulations emphasize the need for clear data usage policies, user consent, the right to access one's data, and the right to be forgotten. They hold organizations accountable for responsibly handling and protecting user data.

Ethical Considerations and Responsible AI

Responsible AI development entails recognizing that data security and privacy are ethical imperatives. Organizations must ensure that AI systems are built with privacy by design, implementing encryption, access controls, and anonymization techniques to safeguard sensitive information. Transparency about data practices and regular audits are essential to maintain user trust.

Conclusion

Data privacy and security in the realm of AI present a delicate balancing act between the promise of technology and the rights of individuals. As AI systems continue to evolve and accumulate data, it is imperative to maintain ethical practices that respect privacy rights. Legislation like GDPR and CCPA serve as important steps towards protecting user data, but organizations must go beyond compliance and prioritize responsible AI development that respects the privacy and security of individuals in the digital age.

4.3 The Role of Humans in AI Decision-Making

Introduction to Human-AI Decision-Making Dynamics

The integration of Artificial Intelligence (AI) in decision-making processes raises complex ethical questions about accountability, responsibility, and transparency. This section delves into the intricate relationship between humans and AI systems in various domains, exploring the challenges posed by autonomous AI decision-making and the measures taken to ensure ethical and responsible AI practices.

Accountability and Responsibility in Autonomous AI

As AI systems gain autonomy in decision-making, questions arise about who should be held accountable for the outcomes. In domains like autonomous vehicles and healthcare, where AI decisions have real-life consequences, defining responsibility becomes crucial. Ensuring that AI systems operate safely and ethically is a shared responsibility involving developers, regulators, and stakeholders.

Explainable AI: Making Decisions Visible and Comprehensible

Explainable AI (XAI) is an evolving field that aims to make AI decisions transparent and comprehensible to humans. XAI techniques provide insights into how AI systems arrive at conclusions, enhancing trust and enabling human experts to intervene when necessary.

This is especially important in critical domains where AI systems might make decisions that impact human lives.

The Controversy of AI Decision-Making Autonomy

The debate over the level of autonomy AI systems should possess in decision-making is ongoing. Striking a balance between human oversight and AI efficiency is challenging. While fully autonomous systems might achieve greater accuracy and speed, the absence of human judgment raises concerns about unforeseen consequences and ethical considerations.

Ethical Considerations and Real-World Examples

Real-world examples underscore the ethical dilemmas posed by AI decision-making. In autonomous vehicles, the "trolley problem" raises questions about how AI systems should navigate life-threatening situations. In healthcare, AI algorithms diagnose diseases and recommend treatments, but the responsibility of final decisions rests with human clinicians.

Building Ethical and Responsible AI

Ethical AI development involves building systems that align with human values and respect fundamental rights. Transparency, fairness, and accountability should be embedded in AI design. Human oversight, especially in high-stakes scenarios, ensures that AI systems make decisions within acceptable ethical boundaries.

Conclusion

The intersection of AI and human decision-making is a complex landscape that requires careful navigation. The ethical considerations, accountability, and transparency surrounding AI decisions are critical to ensure that the integration of AI enhances human well-being without compromising ethical principles. This chapter prompts readers to critically assess the ethical challenges, advocate for responsible AI practices, and contribute to the development of AI systems that empower human decision-making while upholding fundamental values.

CHAPTER 5

AI in Business and Industry

5.1 Automation and Robotics: Transforming Industries with AI

Introduction to Automation and Robotics

Artificial Intelligence (AI) is reshaping industries through the integration of automation and robotics. This section explores how AI technologies are driving innovation in manufacturing, logistics, agriculture, and beyond. It highlights the transformative impact of AI-powered robots on efficiency, productivity, and the workforce.

AI-Powered Robots in Manufacturing

AI-powered robots are revolutionizing manufacturing by streamlining processes, increasing precision, and reducing errors. Robots equipped with computer vision can perform intricate tasks like assembling electronic components with remarkable accuracy. Collaborative robots, or cobots, work alongside human workers, enhancing efficiency in production lines and allowing humans to focus on more complex tasks.

Automation in Logistics and Warehousing

In logistics and warehousing, AI-driven robots are optimizing inventory management, order fulfillment, and goods transportation. Robots equipped with sensors and navigation capabilities autonomously navigate warehouse spaces, picking and packing items efficiently. This automation reduces order processing times, minimizes errors, and ensures timely deliveries.

AI in Agriculture: Precision Farming

In agriculture, AI technologies are transforming farming practices through precision agriculture. Drones equipped with AI and sensors monitor crops, detecting diseases and optimizing irrigation. AI-driven machinery can selectively apply fertilizers and pesticides, minimizing environmental impact and maximizing crop yields. This level of precision increases agricultural efficiency while reducing resource usage.

Impact on the Workforce and Reskilling

The increasing integration of AI-powered automation raises concerns about the future of the workforce. While automation improves efficiency and reduces labor-intensive tasks, it can also lead to job displacement. The workforce of the future will require reskilling and upskilling to adapt to the changing job landscape. Emphasis on acquiring skills that complement AI technologies, such as data analysis and complex problem-solving, is essential.

Ethical Considerations and Societal Implications

As automation and robotics become more prevalent, ethical considerations arise. Ensuring that automation benefits society as a whole, rather than exacerbating inequalities, is crucial. Policies that address job displacement, provide opportunities for reskilling, and ensure fair distribution of benefits are essential to mitigate negative social impacts.

Conclusion

Automation and robotics powered by AI are driving transformative changes across industries, enhancing efficiency, and redefining job roles. While the automation revolution offers immense benefits, it also poses challenges to the workforce. By recognizing the potential of AI-powered automation and preparing for the changing landscape, industries and individuals can harness the power of AI to create a more productive, innovative, and inclusive future.

5.2 Predictive Analytics: Unleashing Future Insights with AI

Introduction to Predictive Analytics

Predictive analytics, fueled by Artificial Intelligence (AI), is a powerful field that harnesses historical data to forecast future outcomes. This section explores how AI algorithms scrutinize data patterns to make accurate predictions, empowering businesses with insights for informed decision-making and resource allocation.

AI Algorithms and Data Patterns

AI algorithms, including machine learning and deep learning models, analyze vast datasets to discern hidden patterns and trends. By identifying correlations and relationships, these algorithms predict future events with remarkable accuracy. This ability to anticipate outcomes enables businesses to make proactive choices rather than reactive responses.

Applications of Predictive Analytics

Predictive analytics finds application across industries. Businesses use it to forecast consumer behavior, enabling targeted marketing campaigns. Financial institutions rely on predictive analytics to anticipate stock market fluctuations and make investment decisions. In healthcare, predictive analytics assists in disease outbreak predictions, supporting timely interventions.

Supply Chain Optimization: AI Transforming Logistics

Introduction to Supply Chain Optimization

This section delves into the revolutionary impact of AI on supply chain management. AI-driven optimization enhances inventory control, demand forecasting, route planning, and distribution strategies, optimizing operations to meet customer needs efficiently.

Inventory Management and Demand Forecasting

AI-driven inventory management ensures that businesses maintain optimal stock levels. AI algorithms analyze historical sales data, external factors like seasonality, and market trends to predict demand. This reduces excess inventory costs while ensuring products are available when customers need them.

Route Planning and Distribution

AI-powered route planning optimizes delivery routes for efficiency and cost-effectiveness. Algorithms consider factors like traffic patterns, weather conditions, and delivery constraints to minimize transportation costs and delivery times. This results in enhanced customer satisfaction and reduced carbon footprint.

Benefits of AI-Driven Supply Chain Optimization

The adoption of AI-driven supply chain optimization leads to substantial benefits. Costs are reduced through efficient resource utilization, distribution, and inventory management. Customer satisfaction improves due to timely deliveries and accurate demand forecasting. Furthermore, sustainability goals are achieved as resource consumption is minimized.

Practical Examples and Case Studies

Real-world examples illustrate the transformative effect of AI in business operations. Companies like Amazon utilize predictive analytics to forecast customer preferences, while Walmart employs AI-driven supply chain optimization to enhance inventory management and reduce waste.

Conclusion

Predictive analytics and AI-driven supply chain optimization exemplify the power of AI to revolutionize business operations. By harnessing historical data to predict future outcomes and optimizing supply chains for efficiency, businesses can make better decisions, enhance customer experiences, and contribute to sustainable practices. The integration of AI into these areas showcases the strategic advantages of embracing technology for growth, innovation, and competitive advantage.

CHAPTER 6

Future Possibilities of AI

6.1 AGI (Artificial General Intelligence): Bridging the Gap to Human-Level Intelligence

Introduction to AGI (Artificial General Intelligence)

This section delves into the fascinating realm of Artificial General Intelligence (AGI), also known as "strong AI." Unlike narrow or specialized AI, which excel at specific tasks, AGI aims to replicate human-like cognitive abilities and versatility across a wide range of tasks. This chapter explores the ambitious goal of achieving human-level intelligence in AI systems.

Human-Like Cognitive Skills and Abilities

The hallmark of AGI is its capacity to exhibit human-like cognitive skills. This includes the ability to reason, learn from experience, understand complex concepts, and apply knowledge to various situations. AGI systems are not limited to pre-defined tasks but possess the adaptability to tackle diverse challenges that humans face.

Challenges of Developing AGI

Creating AGI poses unprecedented technical challenges. AGI systems need to grasp not only the mechanics of problem-solving but also the nuances of human emotions, social interactions, and ethical considerations. Developing algorithms that mimic human cognitive processes demands a deep understanding of human intelligence and consciousness.

Ethical Dilemmas and Societal Implications

The pursuit of AGI brings forth ethical dilemmas. Ensuring that AGI aligns with human values, respects individual autonomy, and avoids unintended consequences is paramount. There are concerns about control: How can we ensure that AGI systems act ethically and make decisions in line with human preferences? Additionally, the impact on employment, societal structures, and human identity raises profound questions.

Prospective Repercussions for Society and Work

The advent of AGI could bring transformative changes to society. On one hand, AGI could revolutionize industries, healthcare, and scientific research, offering solutions to complex problems. On the other hand, it could disrupt the job market by automating tasks currently performed by humans. This underscores the importance of preparing the workforce for shifts in job roles and skills requirements.

AI's Potential for Positive and Negative Impact

The development of AGI presents both utopian and dystopian scenarios. On the positive side, AGI could solve global challenges like climate change, disease eradication, and resource management. However, there are concerns about AGI surpassing human intelligence and control, potentially leading to unintended consequences that humans cannot predict or manage.

Conclusion

Artificial General Intelligence is the pinnacle of AI research, aspiring to create machines that emulate human cognitive abilities. The journey towards AGI is fraught with challenges and ethical considerations. Balancing technological advancements with ethical principles and societal well-being is essential. By understanding the implications of AGI on society, work, and humanity, we can navigate the path to AGI responsibly, harnessing its potential for the greater good while mitigating potential risks.

6.2 AI and Creativity: Navigating the Intersection of Technology and Art

Introduction to AI and Creativity

This section explores the intriguing intersection of AI and creativity, where technology collaborates with human ingenuity to produce art, music, literature, and other forms of creative expression. This chapter delves into the evolving landscape of AI-generated creativity, investigating its possibilities, limitations, and the ongoing debate about the authenticity of AI-generated art.

AI in Creative Production

AI technologies have demonstrated an astonishing ability to mimic and extend human creativity. AI algorithms can compose music, generate artwork, and even write poetry that often blurs the line between human and machine. These tools augment human creativity, offering new avenues for artistic exploration and expression.

Possibilities and Limitations of AI-Driven Creativity

While AI can produce impressive creative works, its creations are often based on patterns and data from existing content. This poses the question: Can AI truly create original and innovative art? Some argue that AI-generated art lacks the genuine emotional depth and conceptual complexity of human-created art. Others see AI as a tool for augmenting human creativity, pushing the boundaries of what's possible.

Collaboration Between Humans and AI

Many artists and creators embrace AI as a collaborator rather than a replacement. They view AI as a source of inspiration, offering novel ideas and perspectives that humans might not have considered. Collaborations between humans and AI have resulted in captivating projects that blend human intuition and AI-driven analysis.

Ethical Challenges in Advancing AI

Loss of Human Control and Superintelligent AI

The development of highly advanced AI systems raises ethical concerns about human control. Superintelligent AI, capable of outperforming humans in virtually every cognitive task, poses risks if it operates without ethical constraints. Ensuring that AI remains aligned with human values and objectives is crucial to prevent unintended consequences.

AI and Human Identity

As AI continues to advance, questions about human identity and value come to the forefront. The integration of AI into daily life could reshape how we perceive ourselves and our relationships with technology. The potential for AI to outperform humans in various tasks might challenge notions of human exceptionalism.

Ethical Governance and Global Cooperation

The ethical challenges posed by AI transcend borders. Responsible AI development requires global cooperation to establish guidelines, regulations, and norms that ensure AI technologies are developed and deployed ethically. Responsible governance is essential to mitigate the risks and promote the benefits of AI technology.

Conclusion

The evolving landscape of AI encompasses both possibilities and uncertainties. From the realm of creative expression to the ethical challenges posed by advanced AI systems, the future of AI holds immense potential and complex ethical dilemmas. By understanding the interplay between AI and creativity and actively engaging in discussions about ethical governance, society can navigate the path forward, harnessing the transformative power of AI while upholding human values and ensuring a positive impact on humanity.

CHAPTER 7

Case Studies in AI

7.1 Self-Driving Cars: Navigating the Road to Autonomous Mobility

Introduction to Self-Driving Cars

This section delves into the revolutionary world of self-driving cars, showcasing how AI applications are transforming the automotive industry. The chapter provides an in-depth examination of the technology behind autonomous vehicles, their potential benefits, and the intricate challenges they pose.

Technology Powering Autonomous Vehicles

Autonomous vehicles rely on a sophisticated blend of AI technologies to navigate and make decisions. Sensor systems, including LiDAR, cameras, and radar, capture real-time data about the vehicle's surroundings. Machine learning algorithms process this data to identify objects, pedestrians, and road signs. Decision-making mechanisms use this information to execute actions such as accelerating, braking, and steering.

Potential Benefits of Self-Driving Cars

Self-driving cars offer a range of potential benefits that could reshape transportation as we know it. Enhanced road safety is a key advantage, as AI systems are designed to minimize human errors that often lead to accidents. Autonomous vehicles could also reduce traffic congestion, optimize fuel efficiency, and make transportation more accessible for people with disabilities or limited mobility.

Challenges and Concerns

Regulatory Frameworks and Ethical Dilemmas

The development of self-driving cars raises complex questions about regulatory frameworks and ethical considerations. How should these vehicles be tested and regulated to ensure safety for all road users? Ethical dilemmas arise, such as programming cars to make life-or-death decisions in emergency situations.

Balancing individual safety, societal benefit, and ethical principles presents a formidable challenge.

Public Acceptance and Trust

The successful adoption of self-driving cars hinges on public acceptance and trust. Convincing individuals to relinquish control to AI systems requires demonstrating their safety and reliability. High-profile accidents involving autonomous vehicles have eroded public confidence, emphasizing the need for transparent testing, rigorous safety standards, and effective communication.

Future Prospects and Real-World Examples

Current Landscape of Autonomous Vehicles

While fully autonomous vehicles are not yet widespread, semi-autonomous features like adaptive cruise control and lane-keeping assist are becoming increasingly common in modern vehicles. These technologies offer a glimpse into the future of self-driving cars and highlight the gradual progression towards full autonomy.

Real-World Deployment and Pilot Programs

Companies like Waymo, Tesla, and Uber have been testing self-driving cars on public roads, collecting data and refining their algorithms. Pilot programs in certain cities showcase the potential benefits of autonomous vehicles, from reduced traffic congestion to improved accessibility for elderly and disabled individuals.

Conclusion

The development of self-driving cars is a significant milestone in the evolution of AI technology. While there are challenges to overcome, from regulatory hurdles to public trust, the potential benefits in terms of road safety, traffic congestion reduction, and enhanced mobility are substantial. By addressing these challenges responsibly and ensuring rigorous testing and regulatory oversight, society can unlock the transformative potential of self-driving cars while prioritizing safety and ethical considerations.

7.2 Chatbots and Virtual Assistants: AI-Powered Communication Tools

Introduction to Chatbots and Virtual Assistants

This section explores the dynamic world of chatbots and virtual assistants, showcasing how AI is revolutionizing communication and interaction between humans and technology. The chapter provides an in-depth analysis of the construction, training, and integration of these AI-driven tools, shedding light on their diverse applications.

Building and Training Chatbots

Chatbots are constructed using Natural Language Processing (NLP) techniques, enabling them to understand and generate human language. NLP algorithms analyze text and context to interpret user queries and generate relevant responses. Chatbots are trained on massive datasets of text to learn language patterns, idioms, and common phrases, allowing them to engage in meaningful conversations.

Applications Across Platforms

Chatbots and virtual assistants are integrated into a wide array of platforms, from websites to messaging apps and smart speakers. They assist users in tasks ranging from customer support inquiries to information retrieval, appointment scheduling, and even entertainment. This versatility makes them a powerful tool for businesses and individuals alike.

Natural Language Processing and Human-Bot Interaction

The success of chatbots hinges on their ability to engage in natural and intuitive conversations. Natural Language Processing algorithms process and understand the nuances of language, including context, tone, and intent. This enables chatbots to provide relevant and coherent responses, creating a seamless user experience.

Real-World Examples of Chatbot Implementation

Customer Support and Service

Companies utilize chatbots to enhance customer support efficiency. Chatbots can provide instant responses to frequently asked questions, troubleshoot technical issues, and guide users through processes like account setup or purchase transactions.

Personal Assistants and Information Retrieval

Virtual assistants like Siri, Google Assistant, and Alexa help users with various tasks, from setting reminders and alarms to answering general knowledge queries. These assistants leverage AI to understand user intent and retrieve relevant information from the web.

Entertainment and Engagement

Chatbots also serve as entertainment tools, engaging users in interactive conversations, storytelling, and games. Some companies create chatbots with unique personalities to entertain users and build brand affinity.

The integration of chatbots and virtual assistants represents a transformative shift in human-computer interaction. These AI-driven tools leverage Natural Language Processing and machine learning to facilitate seamless and personalized conversations. From customer support to personal assistance, chatbots are reshaping the way we communicate with technology. As advancements continue, the potential applications of chatbots are boundless, offering businesses and individuals efficient, engaging, and human-like interactions.

7.3 Image and Video Analysis: Unveiling Insights with AI-Powered Vision

Introduction to Image and Video Analysis

This section immerses us in the world of AI-driven image and video analysis, showcasing how computer vision technology is revolutionizing our ability to extract information from visual input. The chapter provides an in-depth exploration of how AI algorithms can identify objects, scenes, and patterns within images and videos, leading to a myriad of applications across various domains.

AI-Powered Computer Vision

AI-powered computer vision relies on deep learning algorithms that analyze and interpret visual data. Convolutional Neural Networks (CNNs) are a cornerstone of this technology, enabling computers to recognize objects, features, and structures within images and videos. These algorithms learn from vast datasets, gaining the ability to discern subtle distinctions and complex patterns.

Applications of Image and Video Analysis

Face Identification and Recognition

Computer vision technology powers facial recognition systems that can identify individuals from images and videos. This technology finds applications in security, authentication, and even social media platforms where users are tagged automatically.

Object Detection and Scene Understanding

AI can detect and identify objects within images and videos, enabling applications like autonomous vehicles to identify pedestrians, traffic signs, and other vehicles. Scene understanding involves comprehending the context of an image, enabling computers to interpret complex scenes and environments.

Video Surveillance and Anomaly Detection

Computer vision is used in video surveillance to monitor public spaces, detect suspicious behavior, and identify anomalies. AI algorithms can raise alerts in real-time when unusual activities are detected, enhancing security and public safety.

Ethical Considerations and Challenges

Privacy Concerns and Biases

The deployment of AI in image and video analysis raises concerns about privacy and bias. Facial recognition systems, for instance, can infringe upon personal privacy. Additionally, bias in training data can lead to AI systems exhibiting biased behavior, particularly in terms of race and gender.

Case Studies and Real-World Examples

Medical Imaging and Diagnostics

AI-driven image analysis finds applications in medical imaging, assisting doctors in diagnosing diseases from X-rays, MRIs, and CT scans. These systems can help detect early signs of diseases, improving patient outcomes.

Agricultural Monitoring and Crop Analysis

Computer vision is employed in agriculture to monitor crop health, identify pests, and optimize irrigation. Drones equipped with AI-powered cameras capture data that helps farmers make informed decisions for crop management.

Conclusion

AI-powered image and video analysis is unlocking insights from visual data at an unprecedented scale. From facial recognition to medical diagnostics, this technology is reshaping industries and enhancing our understanding of the world. By acknowledging the ethical challenges and leveraging AI responsibly, we can harness its potential to transform businesses, improve processes, and drive innovation across a wide range of fields.

CHAPTER 8

AI Research and Development

8.1 Leading AI Research Institutions: Pioneers of Innovation

Introduction to Leading AI Research Institutions

This section unveils the global leaders in AI research and development, showcasing institutions that have spearheaded groundbreaking contributions to the field. The chapter provides an in-depth exploration of universities, research centers, and tech companies that have driven AI advancements, shedding light on their areas of expertise, notable research endeavors, and collaborative efforts.

Prominent Universities in AI Research

Stanford University

Renowned for its AI research, Stanford has been a key player in shaping the field. The Stanford Artificial Intelligence Lab (SAIL) has contributed to breakthroughs in natural language processing, computer vision, and robotics. Notable alumni, like the creators of Google Brain, have influenced the direction of AI research.

Massachusetts Institute of Technology (MIT)

MIT is a powerhouse in AI research, with its Computer Science and Artificial Intelligence Lab (CSAIL) at the forefront. MIT's work spans various domains, from machine learning to human-computer interaction. Collaborations between academia, industry, and government agencies amplify its impact.

Leading Research Centers and Tech Companies

DeepMind

Acquired by Google in 2014, DeepMind has achieved groundbreaking success in AI research. Known for its advancements in reinforcement learning and neural networks, DeepMind's AI systems have outperformed humans in complex games like Go and StarCraft II.

OpenAI

Dedicated to advancing AI for the betterment of humanity, OpenAI focuses on cutting-edge research and the responsible deployment of AI technologies. It has pioneered research in reinforcement learning, language models, and robotics.

Open Source AI Projects: Democratizing Innovation

Introduction to Open Source AI Projects

This section delves into the open source movement that has democratized AI research and development. The chapter explores how open source projects have played a pivotal role in accelerating AI innovation, fostering knowledge sharing, and empowering collaborative contributions.

TensorFlow: Enabling Scalable Machine Learning

TensorFlow, an open source framework developed by Google, revolutionized machine learning research and application. Its flexible architecture supports a wide range of tasks, from deep learning to natural language processing. TensorFlow's expansive community and rich ecosystem have propelled its adoption across academia and industry.

PyTorch: Facilitating Flexible Deep Learning

PyTorch, an open source library developed by Facebook's AI Research lab (FAIR), gained popularity for its dynamic computation graph and intuitive design. Its ease of use and flexibility have made it a favorite among researchers and practitioners, fueling advancements in deep learning models.

scikit-learn: Empowering Machine Learning Practitioners

scikit-learn is an open source machine learning library for Python that provides essential tools for data preprocessing, model training, and evaluation. Its user-friendly interface and extensive documentation have made it a cornerstone for beginners and experienced practitioners alike.

Conclusion

Leading AI research institutions and open source AI projects have shaped the landscape of artificial intelligence. These entities drive innovation, collaboration, and knowledge dissemination, ensuring that AI technologies are accessible to a global community. By highlighting their contributions, we gain insights into the transformative power of AI research and the democratization of knowledge that underpins its progress.

8.2 Collaborations and Innovations: Fostering AI Advancements through Interdisciplinary Cooperation

Introduction to Collaborations and Innovations

This section delves into the collaborative and interdisciplinary nature of AI research, showcasing how experts from diverse fields converge to drive innovation. The chapter provides a comprehensive exploration of how cross-disciplinary collaboration accelerates AI advancements, leading to novel applications across various sectors.

Interdisciplinary Approach to AI Research

AI research thrives on interdisciplinary collaborations that bring together experts from computer science, neuroscience, linguistics, ethics, and more. These diverse perspectives enrich the field by infusing it with insights from different domains, leading to holistic and innovative solutions.

Cross-Disciplinary Teams and Research

The collaboration between computer scientists, linguists, and cognitive psychologists, for instance, has fueled advancements in natural language processing. Insights from neuroscience have contributed to the development of biologically inspired neural networks, enhancing our understanding of AI systems' learning mechanisms.

Novel Applications of AI Across Sectors

Climate Modeling and Environmental Preservation

AI has found applications in climate modeling, where it processes vast datasets to simulate complex environmental systems. This aids in predicting climate patterns, understanding environmental changes, and formulating strategies for sustainable resource management.

Drug Development and Healthcare

AI accelerates drug discovery by analyzing molecular structures, predicting drug interactions, and identifying potential candidates for further testing. This expedites the development of new therapies and treatments, benefiting healthcare and medical research.

Global Challenges and AI Solutions

AI's ability to analyze large datasets and derive insights has the potential to tackle global challenges like disease outbreaks, poverty, and resource scarcity. AI-driven analytics can provide insights into the spread of infectious diseases, optimize resource allocation, and aid in poverty alleviation efforts.

Value of Collaborations and Cross-Disciplinary Cooperation

Academic Institutions and Research Centers

Leading academic institutions serve as hubs for cross-disciplinary AI research. Collaborative initiatives foster environments where experts can share ideas, methodologies, and findings, leading to transformative breakthroughs.

Open Source Contributions and Community Involvement

Open source AI projects create platforms for collaboration, allowing researchers and practitioners from around the world to contribute code, tools, and insights. This global community-driven approach accelerates innovation and democratizes AI development.

Conclusion

Collaborations and innovations are at the heart of AI research's progress and impact. The collaborative spirit across disciplines has propelled AI to new heights, addressing complex challenges and revolutionizing industries. As we navigate the dynamic landscape of AI research, interdisciplinary teamwork, open source contributions, and the shared pursuit of knowledge remain pivotal in advancing AI's potential to shape technology, society, and the world at large.

CHAPTER 9

The Social Impact of AI

9.1 Job Disruption and Reskilling: Navigating the Transforming Work Landscape

Introduction to Job Disruption and Reskilling

This section delves into the transformative impact of AI on the job market, analyzing the potential effects of automation and AI technologies on various employment roles. The chapter examines how certain job roles are at risk of being replaced and highlights the importance of reskilling and upskilling the workforce to adapt to the evolving job landscape.

Automation and Job Disruption

As AI and automation technologies advance, certain labor roles are vulnerable to replacement. Repetitive tasks that can be automated, such as data entry and routine assembly line work, are at a higher risk. This evolution prompts the need for proactive measures to ensure that workers are equipped with the skills needed for new and emerging job opportunities.

The Need for Reskilling and Upskilling

Reskilling and upskilling are essential components of addressing job disruption. Workers must be provided with training and education that aligns with the demands of new roles in the AI-driven economy. This might involve learning new technical skills, enhancing problem-solving abilities, and developing creativity and adaptability.

9.2 AI in Education: Enhancing Learning Experiences

Introduction to AI in Education

This section explores the transformative potential of AI in education, analyzing how AI-powered solutions can revolutionize the learning experience for students and educators alike. The chapter provides an in-depth examination of how AI can personalize learning, support teachers, and streamline administrative tasks.

Personalized Learning Experiences

AI can analyze individual student data to tailor learning materials and activities to each student's unique needs and learning style. Adaptive learning platforms use AI algorithms to adjust the difficulty and pace of lessons, ensuring that students are engaged and challenged.

Supporting Teachers and Administrators

AI-powered tools can assist teachers in providing targeted support to students who are struggling. Automated grading and assessment systems can reduce teachers' administrative workload, allowing them to focus more on instructional activities and student interactions.

Ethical Considerations and Human Interaction

While AI holds promise for education, it's important to balance technology with human interactions. Maintaining the personal connection between students and teachers and addressing concerns about data privacy and ethical AI use are crucial.

9.3 AI and Socioeconomic Inequalities: Mitigating Disparities

Introduction to AI and Socioeconomic Inequalities

This section explores the potential for AI to exacerbate existing socioeconomic disparities. The chapter delves into how biases in AI algorithms and data can lead to uneven outcomes for marginalized and underrepresented groups. It emphasizes the significance of responsible AI development to ensure equitable access to AI technologies and their benefits.

Biases in AI Algorithms and Data

AI algorithms learn from data, and if the data is biased, the algorithms can perpetuate those biases. This can result in discriminatory outcomes, reinforcing societal inequalities. Efforts to mitigate bias and ensure fairness are crucial to prevent exacerbating disparities.

Responsible AI Development

Developers must proactively address bias and discrimination in AI systems, considering diverse perspectives during design and implementation. Transparency, accountability, and ongoing evaluation are essential to creating AI technologies that serve all members of society equitably.

Conclusion

The complex interplay between AI and social processes underscores the need for thoughtful consideration of AI's societal implications. From job disruption and reskilling to AI's role in education and the potential for socioeconomic disparities, these topics shed light on the transformative power of AI and its challenges. By fostering discussions and understanding, society can navigate the path forward, harnessing AI's potential while ensuring ethical and equitable deployment.

CHAPTER 10

Looking Ahead

10.1 The Evolution of AI: Navigating Future Trajectories

Introduction to the Evolution of AI

This section delves into the exciting realm of potential AI development in the coming years. The chapter explores the multifaceted landscape of AI's evolution, touching on the integration of AI into daily life, advancements in natural language understanding, and the continued growth of machine learning methodologies.

Integration of AI into Everyday Life

AI's influence is projected to become more pervasive, impacting various aspects of daily life. From smart homes and virtual assistants to autonomous vehicles and healthcare diagnostics, AI's seamless integration aims to enhance efficiency, convenience, and personalized experiences.

Advancements in Natural Language Understanding

The evolution of AI is likely to witness remarkable strides in natural language understanding. Chatbots, virtual assistants, and language models are expected to become more proficient at comprehending context, nuances, and even emotions in human language, facilitating more natural and meaningful interactions.

Continued Growth of Machine Learning

Machine learning, the bedrock of AI advancements, is poised to flourish further. With advancements in algorithms, data availability, and computing power, machine learning approaches will become more sophisticated, enabling the development of smarter and more capable AI systems.

Ethical AI Development and the Role of Rules

The chapter also delves into the ethical considerations of AI development. As AI becomes more influential, the need for ethical guidelines becomes crucial. This section explores the importance of defining rules and principles that guide the responsible and ethical development of AI technologies.

Responsible AI Development: Nurturing Ethical and Accountable Systems

Introduction to Responsible AI Development

This section shifts focus to the realm of responsible AI development. The chapter explores concepts and strategies for creating AI systems that are transparent, accountable, and aligned with human values. It emphasizes the necessity of diverse perspectives, ethical problem-solving, and mechanisms for feedback and improvement.

Transparency and Accountability

Creating responsible AI involves ensuring that the inner workings of AI systems are transparent and understandable. When users, stakeholders, and regulators can comprehend how AI systems make decisions, trust is fostered, and accountability is established.

Ethical Considerations and Problem-Solving

AI developers must grapple with ethical dilemmas, such as bias, fairness, and privacy. This section explores the importance of proactive ethical problem-solving, engaging ethicists, and adhering to principles that prioritize human well-being.

Human-Centered Design and Feedback Loops

Incorporating human values and feedback loops are integral to responsible AI development. Creating mechanisms for users to provide input and influence the behavior of AI systems ensures that technology aligns with human needs and values.

Coexistence of Humans and AI: Partners in Progress

Introduction to Coexistence of Humans and AI

This section delves into the symbiotic relationship between humans and AI. The chapter explores scenarios where AI functions not as a replacement but as a collaborator, augmenting human abilities and decision-making across diverse fields.

AI's Role in Healthcare

AI can aid medical professionals by analyzing vast amounts of medical data, assisting in diagnostics, and predicting disease outbreaks. This coexistence between AI and medical experts enhances patient care and medical research.

Cultural Activities and Creative Expression

AI-generated art, music, and literature showcase the potential for humans and AI to collaborate creatively. AI tools assist artists and creators in exploring novel avenues and expanding the boundaries of creative expression.

CONCLUSION

The future landscape of AI is rich with possibilities, innovations, and ethical considerations. By nurturing responsible development, coexisting harmoniously with AI, and addressing ethical challenges, society can harness AI's potential for positive transformation. This chapter encourages readers to envision an AI-infused future while reflecting on the ethical, societal, and human aspects that guide this journey.